A letter from the Author...

Prayer is something people have a very different opinion on. I grew up in church thinking of it as a prompted prayer I had learned. I eventually started calling out to Him like He was my magic genie when life got rough to fix my problem's. I saw as I grew older and grew in my faith, it was something much deeper than what I was familiar with. I now know God love's to hear from us regardless, but he intended us to talk to him as it is a relationship with Him. He wants to hear about our pain, the good things going on in life, our goals, our vulnerability moments and he wants us to love him through it all. I wrote this book for my son, telling him a story one evening, and wanted to teach him more on talking to God with his heart, not just saying a rote type of prayer before bed, and not correcting him when he prayed for his favorite toy, because to a toddler this is important to him right now. Teaching our children early on the foundation of prayer and building a relationship with God is very important. I hope this book can be a light in your walk with the Lord.

Heather

Author: Heather Guidry
Illustrator: Amy Bouquet

ISBN# 979-8-218-56872-6

The Little Cowboy

THAT TALKS TO GOD

This story is dedicated to my lil' cowboy who is already talking to God and praying for others around him, I am so proud of you, and your kind heart.

I pray you never lose sight of having a relationship with God.

-Love Mom

The mornings start early here in Sunflower Valley
for Remington, a young buckaroo who wakes up
before the sun.
Life on a ranch is a full day's work helping with
chores and tending to the animals.

"Good morning God" Remington begins his morning prayer, "I am blessed with another day, no grumble in my belly, and I ask that you help my horse not to stumble, help me be a light to others around me so they will know and love you like I do, Amen."

NEIGHHHH.. .

"Howdy Gunner, are you ready to start another day?"
He asks his horse. Gunner lets out a NEIGH and shakes
his head up and down.

Off to do the chores Remington
begins by tending to the cows...

Fills up water troths...

Brushes the horses...

Collects the chicken eggs...

Cleans up the chicken coop...

Sweeps out the barn and adds fresh hay.

With the chores all finished, he grabs his rope and
throws his lasso at the practice steer.
Loop after loop, swoop after swoop, he gets a little
better each time.
"Well, I'll be! I am blessed to have this talent you've
handed me, Lord. It sure brings me a heap of joy!"
Remington says with a heartfelt grin.

SWOOP!
SWOOP!!

Jennifer, a spunky and curious friend of Remington's runs over to greet him. "Hey there Remington, whatcha doin.?" she asks.

"Hey there, Jennifer," he says, wiping the sweat from his brow. "I'm messin' around with this ol' tractor that just won't fire up. My Pop's showed me a coupla tricks to get it runnin' again, but this one's bein' stubborn."

Jennifer stays by Remington's side, providing him with tools when he needs them, and before long, the machine starts to run smoothly. As they engage in conversation about life, celebrating their success in reviving this old contraption, an unexpected twist in their day occurs...

...clouds start to accumulate, darkening with each fleeting moment. Lightning dances across the sky, while thunderclaps echo through the mountains. The wind howled, toppling a fence that once held the horses in their sanctuary.

"OH NO!" Jennifer exclaims, her voice ringing with urgency. "We gotta gather those horses!" Remington, looking out at the darkening sky, replies gently, "Let's hunker down till this storm blows over, then we can go save 'em." They both duck into the nearby barn, the wind howling like a restless spirit outside.

"In the middle of this rowdy storm, our fence has fallen, and the horses have ran off. Please keep them safe until it's time for their return," Remington chats away with the Big Guy upstairs.
Jennifer raises an eyebrow, her mind confused—he's clearly not chatting with her, so who on earth is he talking to?

As the storm eases up, they gather round to fix the ol' fence, with the last of the clouds rollin' away, they saddle up their horses, feelin' the warmth of the sun peekin' through. With a nod and a gentle nudge, they set their steed and mare into motion, ready to hit the trail and round up the rest of the horses.

"Yee-Haw" Jennifer yells, "We rounded em' all up and back in the fences."
"Thank you for all your help today, Jennifer. I reckon it is time for us to take a lil' break." Remington says to her.

"Woo-Wee! Father, it has been a wild ride of a day, thank you for such a great ranch hand today from my friend Jennifer, and this beautiful view you have given us to remind us all of your glory." Remington says aloud looking off into the distance.

"Who are you talking to Remington?" Jennifer asks with confusion in her voice.

"Well I'm talking to God." Remington says, his smile wide and warm. "It keeps my spirits up and help's me count my blessings, ya know? Life can throw some real curveballs, but I just keep on singin' His praises, even when the storms roll in. I'm mighty grateful for all the little miracles He blesses me with."

"But if you can't see God, how do you know he's there or hears you?" Jennifer asks.
"I can't see the air we breathe, but I sure know it's there, just like I can feel it all around me," Remington says, staring at the horizon. "Now, take a gander at this mighty fine view he's painted. Only the good Lord above could whip up somethin' so beautiful and real." He reaches for his Bible in Gunners saddle bag, and begins to read.

" No one has ever seen God; but if we love one another, God lives in us, and his love is made complete in us. 1 John 4:12" He reads aloud.
"Also, Isiah 40: 26. Look up and see! Who created these? He brings out the stars by number; He calls all of them by name. Because of his great power and strength, not one of them are missing."

"Now, if that same God who flung the stars into the night sky and knows 'em all by name took the time to create folks like you and me, well shoot, that's somethin' to ponder on. It makes me wanna connect with Him every single day, like sittin' on the porch sippin' on sweet tea, just chattin' away with Him."

Jennifer sat there, soaking in every word he read, her mind started to wonder like a tumbleweed in the wind. She felt gratitude for Remington, who had made the day so special. "Thank you, Remington," she said with a smile. "I must head home. See ya later."
As she walked away, the night air wrapped around her, and thoughts of their conversation danced in her head. She thought over the stories he'd shared about God, the kind of wisdom that felt like a gentle nudge from above. It was a moment she'd remember forever.

She begins to talk aloud...

"Hey there, God. it's me Jennifer." She begins to say, "I want to say how thankful I am for my friend Remington. It's become real clear to me that you're always right there with me, no matter where life takes me, through the good and the tough times I'll have to face. Help me share your goodness for others, just like Remington has done for me today. Goodnight, God. Can't wait to chat again tomorrow."

THE END
SEE YA LATER FOLKS